OF ALL THE STARS,
THE EVENING STAR

Real and Fictional Latin Women Poets

Also by Jim Levy

Nonfiction
Corazón (and Merkle)

Poetry
Cooler Than October Sunlight
The Poems of Caius Herennius Felix
Monet's Eyes
Seen From A Distance

Essays
Joy to Come

Memoirs
The Fifth Season
Rowdy's Boy
Those Were the Days (with Phaedra Greenwood)

Travel and Fiction
Mar Egeo

OF ALL THE STARS, THE EVENING STAR

Real and Fictional Latin Women Poets

Jim Levy

Atalaya Press

Atalaya Press

Printed in the United States of America

ISBN: 978-1-7337940-3-9

*For A. S. Kline, creator of Poetry in Translation, a web site of
original and translated poetry*

CONTENTS

AUTHOR'S NOTE

One day in May, which sounds like the first line of a memoir, I was reading the poems of Sulpicia, the only woman Roman poet whose work has survived, and found them to be fresh, direct and defiant. When her uncle tells her that she is to accompany him to his farm in central Italy, she resists, explaining that she would prefer to stay in Rome with her lover. In the next poem, her uncle relents and she rejoices. Then her lover jilts her for a lower-class woman, and she gets sick and suffers.

I wished that more than six of her poems had survived and so I decided to write a poem or two in her voice, in so far as such a thing is possible. I imagined that a year after losing her lover, on her twenty-second birthday, she accepts her uncle's invitation, goes to his farm, and discovers that she loves the country, especially the animals and the bees. She falls in love with the son of a neighboring farmer.

I was seventy-seven when I read Sulpicia's poems and having spent a lifetime writing books about myself or in my voice, I was tired of myself. If I could write a poem from Sulpicia's point of view, why stop there? I decided to give voice to the women of the Latin poets: Catullus' Lesbia, Propertius' Cynthia, Tibullus' Delia, Horace's Lydia and Ovid's Corinna. For the fun of it, I threw in Caius Herennius Felix's Paccia, although Herennius and Paccia are fictional characters in one of my earlier books.

After writing about a dozen poems from the women's point of view, I became excited about the concept of the book. It would stretch my imagination, challenge my assumptions, reveal my inner femininity. After years of obsessing about death, perhaps I wanted to give birth. The book grew and grew, and the women became so real to me that for much of the day, I lived in their world.

Coming to the end, I have no illusions. At best, these poems are by a man trying to sound like various women. For that matter, does a woman sound different from a man? In many cases, no. Nevertheless, for over two thousand years the Latin poets have had their say about love and hate and sex and marriage, and to be frank, I am tired of them too. If readers can get past the weirdness of this book and enjoy it for what it is, an old man's attempt to inhabit the life and minds of women who lived 2000 years ago, they have my gratitude. I offer it with humility to the women in my life, who gave me life in more ways than one.

Jim Levy
September 2019
Arroyo Hondo, New Mexico

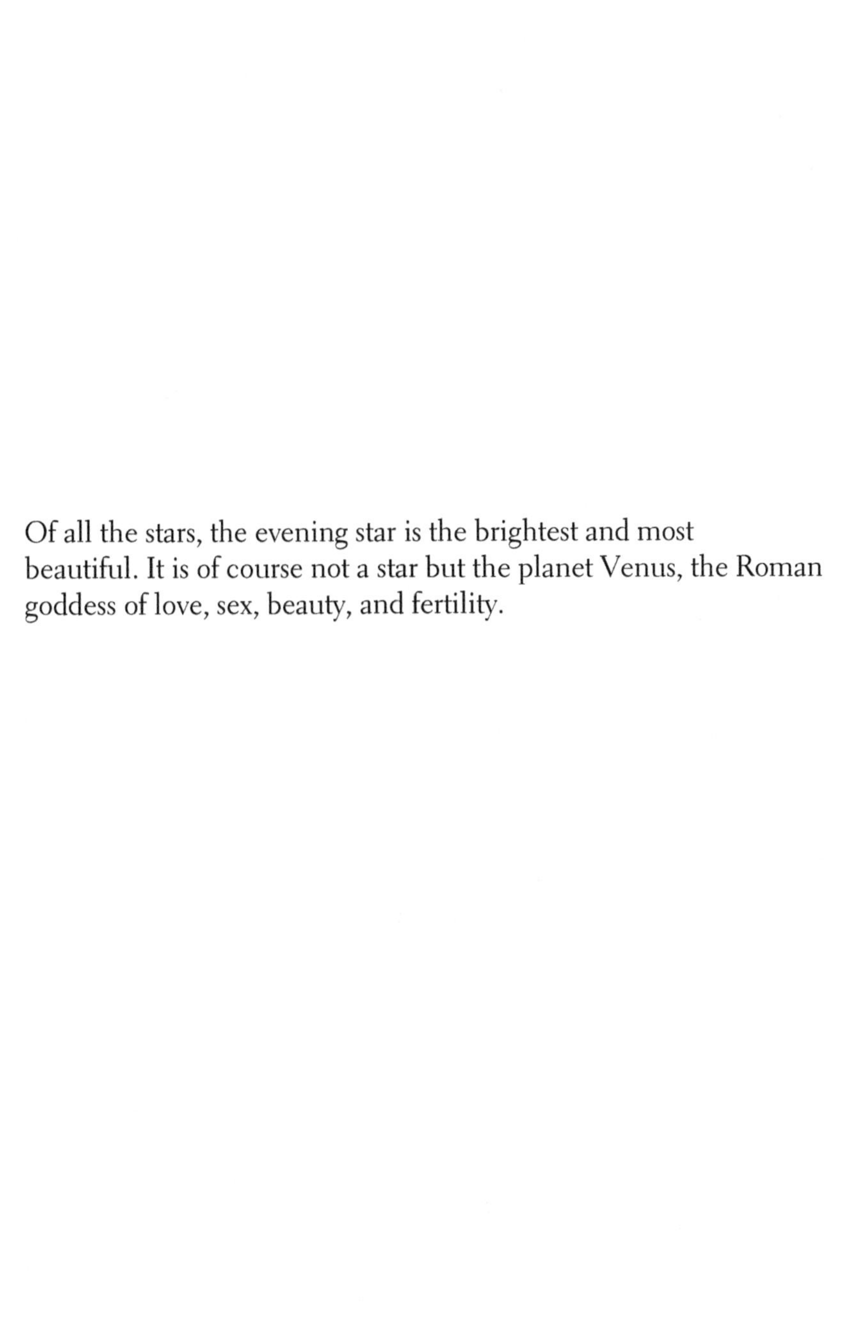

Of all the stars, the evening star is the brightest and most beautiful. It is of course not a star but the planet Venus, the Roman goddess of love, sex, beauty, and fertility.

LESBIA

Lesbia recalls meeting Catullus

That night you came and dined with us
there was a wind, then soft rain.
My hair was dressed by Aemilia
who does it to perfection, and I wore no jewelry
except the brooch my husband gave me.
When I barked at you he laughed thinking
I was scornful of your youth.

I barked – and burned. The spark was there.
Some call it love, an arrow or an illness,
a misfortune not to be evaded.
I don't call it anything but strange.
Why one and not another? Dear boy,
I said to you that night, *love is not a wound.*
You thought I meant to lure you with those words
and so, to end the evening, you read a poem by Sappho.

> *The sweet murmur of your voice*
> *makes my heart beat faster.*
> *One glance from you and I can't speak.*
> *A thin flame slides beneath my skin,*
> *cold sweat trickles down my back,*
> *I turn pale as dry grass.*

Of course I knew that poem
and knew you left off both the start
and end of it, to hide what you were saying
and to whom.

Lesbia questions Catullus

It's true, I curse you off and on to friends and servants,
the ones who know to keep their mouths shut,
but that just proves how fond I am of you,
your languid northern drawl and curly fragrant hair,
your lazy eye that looks at me with love.
Fond of you and more.
I would bake you if I thought
you'd rise to the occasion.
But your poems, they make you suspect,
swearing passion, cursing, sardonic digs
at me and even at your friends.
Just who are you, and are you up for this,
real love with a real woman?

Lesbia's good manners

Please thank Manlius who lends his house
for us to meet. He makes sure the floors are swept,
the rooms are sprinkled with perfumed water from a spring.
It's still a dump – there's a tortoise in the courtyard
and the fountains have no water. Yet you make me
welcome with flowers and a cake and figs and wine,
and best of all, a separate room for me to bathe,
dress my hair and restore my makeup.

To tell the truth, that first time I was bored,
but boredom led to something better, a wicked
impulse to excite you, you
my comely boy, afraid but cocky, sitting
on the bed. And I admit
we smashed those pillows, didn't we,
we made that bed of oak groan with love.
So don't forget to thank good bachelor Manlius.

Lesbia's makeup

You say you prefer my face naked
without any makeup. Do you think
these round dark oxen eyes
are given me by nature? Foolish man,
my naked face is course and wrinkled,
reddened by the brassy sun.

If you're good I'll leave the door ajar
 and let you watch the magic of Aemilia.
She parts my hair, divides it into sections,
clips a little, the curls fall to my lap.
She takes an ivory comb and combs each lock.
Then she lines the bottles up, ochre, saffron, chalk,
and with her fingertips she blends them
and applies them to my face.
I hold my mirror up and turn it
this way, that way to see the progress of her alchemy.
At each step I reward her with a cube
of quince paste – I pop it in her mouth,
but if she missteps, I jab her with a hairpin.
She lines the brows with kajal
mixed with soot. Lashes should be long, dark and curly
and she does it using cork that's lightly burnt,
and finally lines the eyes with kohl
or malachite. The end result is me
whom you think artless.

Lesbia sets the record straight

Why call me Lesbia? Lesbia who? Never heard of her.
A shepherdess perhaps or one of Sappho's girls?
Everyone knows she's me because you
used my brother's name in that poem about us.
So go ahead, use my real name: Lady Clodia Pulchra.
Don't use Metelli, stick with Pulchra.

Lesbia writes to Catullus from Baiae

When here I miss the city, in the city
I miss Baiae's baths and murals,
the taste of sun-soaked melons
and honeyed wine chilled with snow.
Dear, you think it's wicked, but it isn't.
It's true I swim at dawn naked
as a newborn calf but after that,
at noon, a light meal –
a salad and some simple seafood,
then a walk among the pines
and a good long soaking
in the thermal springs.
I have a nap followed by a dinner
in the old mode, men first,
women present only in the second half
and not reclining
– maybe mullet caught off Corsica
and shrimp walled in with asparagus.
Dusk glows on the roses.
A nighttime concert. Afterwards
blossoms of wild pear fill the night.
I read your poems
and hold you in my heart.

Lesbia admonishes Catullus

You mock my sparrow
who hopped here, there and everywhere
and nipped my fingers,
my little bird whose name you don't remember,
which would be fine
except you mock him
to your cronies at the Club
and now my name is scrawled on city walls
by sausage vendors.

You mock him and what's worse,
you mock his death with phony tears,
but it is you, not death, who feeds
on every little pretty thing.
His name was Liber, the god the plebs
worship for his wine and freedom.
Now that you know,
you can call him by his name.

Lesbia, in a bad mood, discusses his poetry

I'm not some filthy slut
who calls your poems
a joke; I like them.
But here's advice,
take it or ignore it:
You lard a poem with myths
that weigh it down; half
the young no longer know them.
In the next poem you introduce a talking door.
Do doors talk in Verona?
You use diminutives to excess,
little this and little that,
perhaps some little thing
is worrisome to you.
Virgil wrote of agriculture,
Lucretius physics,
you count our kisses –
a thousand, hundred, hundred thousand kisses kissed,
too many kisses to account for.
For you breezes are like overdrafts,
kisses coins, and lost investments
are like losing love.
You probably count the napkins after dinner.
As for metrics, I'm old fashioned,
prefer the epic beats and elegiac,
not the polymetrics and the tricky
new ones you employ.
You steal from Callimachus
and from Sappho too.
Worst of all you mix artifice and feeling.
It's time you found a manly voice
to speak of love and pleasure
as we know it, not from some book

Lesbia remembers offering a gift

Remember, early on I offered you some money
to fill your purse and chase the spiders out.
You stole that line and other scrapes of wit
I gave you free of charge.
You refused the money, saying you were
not for rent. Stupid man,
I wasn't buying or rewarding you
or doing anything except showing you my love.
It was a gift! A gift, which means the same as – never mind.
You declined the coins so you could write
of poverty and grief. Good for you.
Go down in history as a genius and a fool.

Lesbia explains some things to Catullus

It makes me cross when you crucify yourself
between the poles of love and hate.
I love. It's you who hate.
I loved you and still love you.
Your shtick is simply Sappho's
about true love's bitter sweetness.
There's no need. We love as lovers
love, not as spouses trapped in wedlock.
We had our time and now's the time
to forget the bad and praise the love
between a poet and his true love
whom you call Lesbia.

Lesbia quotes Catullus

The sun sets
why do poets say the obvious?
and *it rises in the morning*
yes and
death is forever.

Is it your death or mine you mourn?
You wet your brother's ashes with your tears.
Since then you've grown to be a man
for it is death not love that makes a boy a man.

Lesbia speaks about Catullus' marriage poem

I cried that you could write such touching lines
about a feast and choral songs, the bride, fourteen,
in saffron cloak, who goes from mother's
arms to groom's, the procession to his house
arm in arm, pelted by nuts thrown by boys
who joke about the wedding bed
where in wedlock the bride and groom embrace.

But
your marriage poem is not for me.
Weddings are for joining gold or healing feuds.
You and I were flowers on the meadow's edge
gently touched by sun and rain,
grazed by a plow that didn't even see us.

Lesbia ends it

I did tell you l loved you and I did,
and I did tell you that it would last
and I meant that too,
but I thought you knew I meant it
merely as a token of my love.

I was not your girl, neither yours nor girl.
The sun shone brightly for a day.
Our love, our misdeeds, were graffiti
scrubbed off the bathhouse walls
by my brother's henchmen.

I won't waste my tears on you.
You were the least of my losses.
Yet you are here, in my heart
the young man who set the world on fire.

Lesbia/Clodia refutes Cicero

I am not a toad and you'll never see my breasts.
You called me many ugly things,
a sorry bitch, drinker, gambler, fornicator.
Bitch, okay at times, but never sorry,
my sins not of the flesh
but of the heart, a coldness
where once there was a fire.

Since the State won't let me
have a private life,
I proclaim that I am Claudia Metelli,
of the Claudii Pulchii clans,
mother of Caecilia Metelli,
true love of Gaius Valerius Catullus of Verona.

Delia, Nemesis and Pholoe

Delia has doubts about country life

You call me gorgeous,
                blond, blue-eyed.
Any girl would like to hear that
                but please, Tibullus, be more specific.
                Are my hands as soft
                                and white as linen?
Am I as graceful as that nymph with sea-green
                hair who rides a fish?
                I will say this:
                I'm not a girl who carries water
                                in a leaky vessel
        or who hatchets her old husband
                        on their wedding night.

        You talked of waters
singing lullabies
        and kicking off our shoes to dance
in meadows decked with flowers,
                the quiet life, with humble earthenware
        and rustic beds.
Cupid himself, you said, was born
        among the lambs and corn

        but instead I find vast fields
plowed by slaves with oxen,
        and cows with swollen udders eating apples
in the orchard
        and at night, the groans of bears
around the sheepfold.

You're not poor, despite your cries
                of poverty

and not as honest as you claim.
        That accessory for instance
cost a fortune, and that dye
    barely covers streaks of gray.

I tried to tell you, Tib,
     the country's not for me.
          I'm not attractive here,
in clothes laid out on rocks to dry,
    my hands reddened by the sun,
     my dainty shoes spattered
            with sheep shit.

I'd rather visit briefly in the fall,
    two weeks at most, when the air is cool
and sweetened by a turkey or a pig
    cooking in a pit
  and green is bruised to gold
       and fruits are ripened by the autumn sun.

Delia advises Tibullus

Let's be ourselves,
          you go and woo that gorgeous boy
    whose white limbs haunt your dreams.
I'll return to Rome and that soldier
            riding boldly across the training grounds
   or to that merchant selling perfumes
                from Armenia.
You and I can still be friends.

Water your plants
          love the roses
spend your assets on some stud
              or go bed Marathus;
         no one minds.
He's prettier than me (and vainer).
          Enlist Priapus and his scythe
   to cut down his resistance.
He has a bold panache and tender cheeks.

      But be patient when you woo him.
Horses only slowly learn to love the bridle.
              Intoxicate him with the fumes
of love and you can mold him over time
       to suit your needs
                and to esteem the muse above gold gifts.

Delia wakes up to the truth

You needn't worry Tib,
I'll stay chaste.
I have no choice.
I'll never know a man's light touch
or rough because
like Echo, I can't speak but wait
for you to speak.
My boyfriends, husband, lovers,
even me
are phantoms of your mind, puppets
made of silken hair and pupils
flecked with yellow marble.
You pull the strings; we hop.
I am a woman made of mist,
a name that fits the meter,
a ghost that serves the genre.
Better that I guess
than never having lived
but I would wander off the page
and live a life.

Nemesis says ignore signs at your risk

You scoff at how the sacred chickens eat
and what, a pink quartz in their crops,
but when Pompey laughed and had one
thrown into the sea, he lost the battle
that the chicken said he'd lose.

Flights of annual cranes,
the significance of thunderclaps, comets
that portend a rise to heaven or a fall from power:
we see in signs disasters or a happy union.
Livers, songbirds, sets: you dismiss them
as the need to understand
what can't be understood,
but Antony and his queen ignored them
and were lost, first to love, then to Caesar.

Nemesis reveals her true nature

Don't look away Tibullus; unlike Delia
I am real. Put aside your poses
and pretensions and the puppets
that you string along.
I'm the dusky lover you resist
who bears the gifts of my affection.

You have good looks, your health and wealth,
a privileged place by birth,
and yet you have suspicions, don't you,
intimations of white hair, loose flesh, a mind
spongy with unsubtle thoughts,
so embrace the one who waits for you,
so come and be my love.

Nemesis sums up

A hissing snake nests on your grave
and hatches tiny hissing things.
The boatman checks you off like freight
and takes you to the misty underworld
that snatches all things in the end,
where three gods oversee your soul
that flies around, a bat,
or stands eternally bewildered, lost.

It's all a myth. We come from Chaos
as the spawn of Chance
and live a life of sorrow.
The blind sun blinds us
and the sighted moon can't see us.
Our beds are pyres and we return
to Nothing, understanding nothing
of our birth or death or what's transpired.

Prohoe advises a young man and his buddies

Stop! Fighting!
You're no better than barbarians.
You drink new wine too fast
and look what happens: brawling kicks
and blows and sobs and bloody faces.
Even Bacchus turns away, disgusted.

Tell us, wretched boy, about your wound,
love's arrow sent unerring to your heart.
Don't drink another drop
until you've told us all about it. There's no shame
in loving. We're sure that she, or he, is noble.

You poor dog, there's no witch
with magic sauce, no god to intercede.
You're in the undertow of violent love
that drags you out to where a serpent
wraps her coils around you
and . . . you know the rest,
a bad death in the waves, far from land.

Pholoe answers Tibullus

Don't lecture me Tibullus, stop with the warnings.
I'll love as I please, and whom.
I'll be as soft or hard, sweet or cruel as I see fit.

Venus herself has flogged me with her lessons,
how to leave one bed for another,
how to pick the lock of a young heart
and the pocket of an old one.
A girl must use her youth while she is young,
and use the youths while they are young
and pluck the old men naked.
The price youth pays is heartbreak,
while old men pay in pearls and coin.

I don't doll up my face with blush
or coif my hair or even clip my nails.
I don't plump up my freckled breasts.
The rustic look – that's my art,
to present myself as unadorned
and cool. Indifference breeds devotion.
I mind my words and hide my thoughts.
Love scorches those who fly too close
and leaves untouched the boys and girls
who merely play the game.

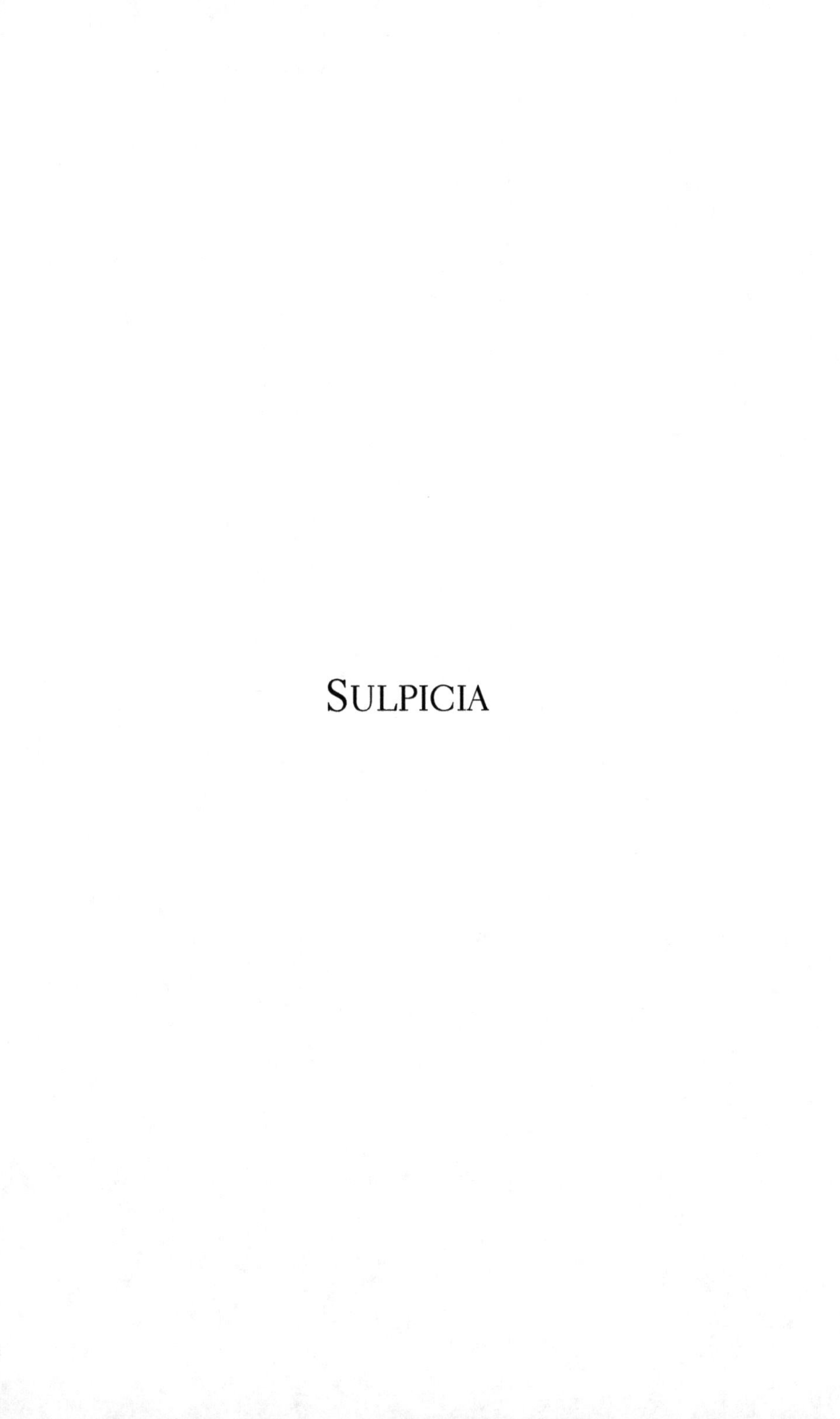

SULPICIA

Sulpicia asks Cerinthus

Am I your only love
          in the whole wide world?
Am I the only object of your gaze?
When passion rises in your heart
          is it for me
                    only me?

That's what you told me.
                    Is it true?

Sulpicia chastises Cerinthus

Cerinthus, you missed my birthday
and you missed your chance
to love a loving girl.
You threw the dice; they came up ones.
Your soul detached from common sense
and sweetness lost its bet to lust. You played me,
then went sniffing like a hound
for a common girl who wears
a simple dress but isn't simple, is she?
She enslaved you with her voice and jet-black hair,
but was it just for coin? It's a gamble,
for a man can never know for sure.
She's beneath you, not like me,
Servius' daughter, niece of Messalla,
from a family that doesn't mix white
with red or eat without a knife and spoon.

Sulpicia goes to her uncle's farm in central Italy

It's May and all is growing, glowing, spurting up.
    Fuzzy chicks are running in the yard, and fattened
piglets are sucking on their mother's milk.
    Kids with foreheads swelling with first horns
clash and race, finches storm the thorny bushes,
    rooks repeat their calls, deer come close
and stare at me. I stand still and stare at them!

And the bees! The honeybees! Not tame ones housed in boxes
but wild bees that live in tunnels underground
    and in caverns of decaying trees.
They emerge at dawn to fill the summer air with humming joy.
    They assault wild thyme, beds of violets, rosemary,
bruised balm, rank savory, and parsley's humble herb,
    then when tired they sink down to sip
the surfaces of ponds and streams.
    At day's end they fly home in flights that sparkle
in the sun and pack their hives with drops of gold.

Sulpicia recounts a day with her new lover, the son of a local landowner.

Thank you Venus. This time you have kept your promise
with a country lad, a generous lover, worthy of my trust.
This time goddess, you have blessed each day
with the sweetness of true love.
While I write poems and practice on the lyre,
he drains a marsh, breeds mules,
or grafts young vines and sets new lime trees
near the river. We spend our afternoons together
in the garden where a statue of Priapus stands,
his large scythe raised to frighten birds and thieves.
The stream runs by and water snakes slip harmlessly
among the mossy weeds. A wild olive shades the grass
we crush down with our love.
Afterwards we gather roses that will bloom again.
In the evening, we drink young wine
and listen to the wind that shakes the shutters.
When the room gets cold
he falls asleep, I lie awake,
my naked soul too hot to touch.

Sulpicia is proud of her love

No shy girl me, not this time, this time
I proclaim my love, let it be seen,
let me be heard, and rumor be my rapture,
innuendo be my pride. News of us
brings only celebration. I don't lie,
I have witnesses: two frogs, the weeping willow,
and the snake's eggs – they all saw
that this is real, not blind dream,
and slander cannot touch us.

Sulpicia and her love

He pulled the covers down.
Amazing how he never tires
of gazing on his naked girl
and then day dawned.

I think I'd gaze forever
on his smooth white flesh.
The moon was up,
its gleam played tricks on me
and then day dawned.

Some morning I won't have to leave,
he cried. He kissed me and we slept
and then he woke and wept.
I kissed his tears away
and quieted his cry
and then day dawned.

Sulpicia's lover is conscripted into the army

O take me with you, bring me with you to the camp,
tell your captain I am just some slut
who trails the troops
and you will have a girl to comfort you,
a girl for fair and dark days.
I'll follow you the way that dead girl
followed her poet up toward the light.
I'll arm myself and strike a blow for you.
At night I'll be your queen of love.

You promised me. You said a lie.
You promised we would always be together.
You said you'd be here when the sheep were born.
I whistled for you and in reply, a bleating lamb.

You promised me a thing that's hard,
to love me til the lime trees grow to fullness
and the limes taste sweet.

You promised me. You lied.

CYNTHIA

Propertius comes home and finds Cynthia sleeping

Drunk, on the street, slaves waving torches
to lead me home, I staggered in to find her
sleeping like that girl who woke up lonely
on the beach and saw her lover's ship
a distant speck, or that other girl
who when wasted from orgiastic dancing
collapsed and passed out on the grass.
So my Cynthia, her head resting on her
puffy hand,
>   *breathing softly.*

I was moved to see her sleeping
through the hours that were meant for us,
and slid a straying curl from off her face,
and now aroused, urged on by wine and love,
twin instigators of my lust, contending
>   *with my rectitude*
and yet agreeing she is mine to have,
I pressed against her, leaned down to kiss her,
>   *to fondle what I so adored*

. . . but did I dare disturb her? What if she dreamed
I was a stranger come to hurt her.
I stood transfixed; I feared to rouse her rage.
Befuddled now, what should I do?
Then she stirred. Not I but moonlight
from the window kissed her eyes.
She sighed, sat up
>   *and spoke:*

You prick. Where have you been?
Did that slut evict you from her bed
and slam the door on you?
Is that her stink on you?
You lurch in here, lit up.
What time is it? Limp now are you?
You thoughtless bastard.
I waited, weaving, singing,
lonely, weary, finally slept
to have you wake me up, your eyes glazed with drink
and mine red and swollen, uglier than muck.
My tears are not for you, you lush, they're for me.

Cynthia talks to Propertius

You wonder how it is I love a man like you
who screams at me and calls me names.
It's not because of Venus or Apollo.
It's the way you linger at the door,
then enter swiftly, light, quick as a thief.
And the lock of dark hair over your eyes,
those poet eyes both dark and bright. pupils blue.
I even like your gamey smell and ink-stained fingers
that gently touch my waist,
and when we struggle to the sound of hissing silk,
I am a slave to love and branded such.
You rip my shirt. We lie together,
dry twigs catching fire.
Most of all, I love how solemnly you state your case,
how love like ours is like a swollen river
that overflows its banks
and floods the world with joy.

Cynthia goads Propertius

Sextus, it wears me out, how, if I attend
a party, you show up for the main course,
if I hold forth you stick your nose in
with a witty quip or worse, a poem.
If I act the fool you are doubly stupid
and when I'm stuck in Rome you are off
to Umbria, oh, your lovely Assisi.

If you persist in this behavior,
love, I'll wear *you* out
since, let's face it, I'm the prod
and you're the ox.

Cynthia posing (sarcastically) as a Roman aristocrat

When there I miss the city, in the city
I miss Baiae's baths and morals,
the sight of sun-soaked matrons
and their portly men.
Dear, you think it's wicked, but it isn't.
It's Ostia that's wicked; have you been there,
to the dockside brothels where you can get
two women for the price of one
and wine that's laced with dirty spices
and opium for sleep and dreaming.
That's not Baiae, my darling,
Baiae is ritzy. You'll see;
I'll come back changed, more refined,
refreshed. with less flesh.

I swim at dawn naked as a pebble.
At noon, a light meal – chickpeas
and some crab or eel,
then a walk among the pines
and a good long soaking
in the thermal springs
except the Sulphur – it fouls my hair,
then a nap followed by a dinner:
purple carrots and a hare caught
in the trapline weeks ago
and we'll invite the local wit
who will demonstrate his art
of begging for a crust
and sponging off the rich.
A nighttime concert – crickets shrieking,
and to bed, alone of course,
your poems sticking in my head.

Cynthia on marriage

The laws have been lifted and you rejoice
that you don't have to marry some tiresome maiden.
You can now love as you please.
You can marry me.
        So where's the ring?

I won't hold you back. Go plunder an entire province
for its silver, slaves, girls, whatever you can put your hands on,
and then I'll give you what you want: a pledge.
I'll enslave your spirit in the same way I've enslaved your flesh
        when we marry.

You tell me how you won't have sons.
That's what you said:
      No bones and hair and flesh
      of mine will be a tasty morsel for a spear
      or the main meal for a sword.

Such eloquence avoids the fact that you're
        afraid of marriage.

Cynthia rebukes Propertius

You harp on death, usually mine,
sometimes yours –
death, death: you do go on about it
and I see you on the beach, blackened
by the sun, seaweed clinging to your hair.
I'm sick of it and sick of you telling
me you love me and rushing off
to write it down and shout it
to the crowd that hangs around your patron.
Your love is like the tide
that floats in shells and driftwood
and drags them out again.

I'll say this about your poems,
they're honest to a fault.
They let the horror of our love shine through.
They've served their purpose,
emblazoned us as cruel and weak
and razed our reputations.
You should put them to the torch
and cease to ride them for your fame.

If you really care so much, go to the Anio
where it gushes down the hillside
to the fields of corn, and plant there a plain pillar:

> *Here lies golden Cynthia*
> *her glory has been wedded to this soil.*

Cynthia returns from Naples early

I burst in and saw it all, one glance was enough
in a back room of our favorite tavern, musicians
in the corner silenced by my look,
and your servant with stubby arms
passed out behind the couch
and your silly drunken whores
with painted faces smeared with wine
and of course Yourself the Coward shocked
to see me back in Rome, a bare breast in your hand,
and bits of halibut and poppies in your hair
and broken crystal on the floor.

Quite the party! You all looked scared,
your faces ashen as if I'd come to sack the city
or was Odysseus returned from Troy to have a word
or two with the woeful men who eyed his wife.
The lamp fell over, the table overturned,
the girls ran for it, I know them,
I won't name them,
one lives with colosseum cats near the Gardens
and the other one farts through silk
and the third has a face like a ship's beak.
I felt contempt, and anger, milk seething in a pan.
I fumed and raged and spat.
My hair was wild, my eyes were sparking.
Need I say it:
I looked good.

Cynthia writes to Propertius

Dear,
    it isn't witchcraft that's turned me cold.
        You've earned this.
You've injured me in many ways.
You sneak around with women,
      you make me cry.
You compare me to Penelope
      and find me wanting,
how she used her guile to trick the suitors
and stay pure. I think she was a prude
      and probably frigid.

    My eyes seduced you? Fool.
You forget that first time
      when you paid me,
you weren't sure where to put the money,
      in my hand or on the table.
      Afterward
you called love *evil*
      – such an ugly word, a word
for that which women do in order to survive.
As for love, *that* word:
I'd slip a noose around its neck
      and string it up.

You thought I'd sob and ask an augur
      for a sign?
You thought I would forgive?
          Return to you?
      Damned if I will.

I hate to be the one to tell you –
        you're uncouth.
It's true, my mother lived above a wine shop
            three flights up,
        but I'm an educated girl
while you, you're Etruscan to the core,
flighty, devious and crude.

Does this letter tell you anything
        you didn't know?

        Yours, no longer,
                Cynthia

Cynthia's return

Ghosts do exist. After the cremation
something survived, call it shade or spirit.
I tossed and closed my eyes; perhaps I slept.
Then Cynthia, thin as a cancerous cat, leaned over me;
her dress was singed, her scorched lips cracked.
She snapped her brittle finger
and she spoke:

Are you asleep? The sleep that spent lovers
sleep, exhausted by their feats of love?
Have you forgotten our midnight antics
in the slums of sunless Subura,
how I climbed through the window and down a rope
and dangled dancing in the air
while you laughed below, looking up my dress?
We would find an alley or a wall or lay our cloaks down
and do it in a ditch like dogs as if passersby were blind.

What happened to me? Ask Lygdamus,
first among my slaves, who handed me the wine
he'd spiked with treason, use your best persuasion
and the white hot tongs to get him to confess,
and that nomad slave, who used her day off
turning tricks for pennies, ask *her* how it is
she wears expensive clothes with hems
that sweep the streets she used to work.
Explain to her she needs to talk,
hand her a burning dish until she does.
And if you can, intercede for poor old Petal
who is hung up by her hair because
she dared to say my name

and ask to be there at my funeral
where, maybe I missed it, did someone see you there
in your dark gray best stained with tears?
Did you pull your hair and shriek with grief?
Was it too much to ask, that you follow me
outside the city and sprinkle spices on the flames
and smash a jar the way true lovers should?
You think I didn't know, being dead,
that no one lingered by my corpse a day
to ward off evil spirits with a rattle.

If *you* had died I would have wandered
with my mind quite gone with grief,
and scratched my face. I'd collect your bones
and raise a stone that bore your name
and press my breast upon that stone.
Instead you live and other women have you now
but I shall have you soon enough.
We'll grind our bones together in such passion
as we ground our flesh, until they're dust.

PACCIA

Paccia Glycera writes to Caius Herennius Felix

Dear Caius,
I thought of you last night, about the morning when a low fog
blanketed the town and we were high above the ghostly world
and listened to the slapping of the sea against the pilings
and the sad voice of a vendor praising his fresh fish.

I crossed the shining sea and it was smooth
and safe. Five days with other girls to Sicily
and up the coast to Ostia and Rome
where I joined my aunt in Subura.
I settled in a neighborhood where Spanish-born collect,
on a block of mainly Gades folk.

I joined a troupe and we performed the canto hondo
and the dances that we learned from those who live
in caves in southern Spain. Well-born Romans
have an appetite for them and paid us well.
I met my husband, lead guitar and secretary
of the music guild. He's from Sanlúcar
and has himself some gypsy blood.
Marcus taught me how to read and write;
we have a lovely girl and lovely son.
A third, our sweet Flacilla, died at two,
her dust placed in a tiny urn.
We both gave up our music, I to be a mother,
he a porter for the merchant on the second floor.

Please write to me and tell me you are well.
If you do, I'll write back
and tell you, you must wonder, why I left.

Sincerely Yours,
     Paccia Glycera Valerius

Paccia describes Subura

Dear Caius,
So glad you've written me about your life,
so very glad you're well. Gades sounds as dull as ever.
As for Rome, it's ten times Gades,
and you were right about Subura,
it's dirty, crowded, boiling hot in summer
and at night, we hear the shrieks of pimps
and the sobs of gaudy smelly girls
and the squeal of ungreased axles
as the last wagons rumble out of town.

But alive! Royal trumpets day and night,
and people teeming the narrow lanes and wide avenues
and senators rolling by high above the mob
and slaves galloping after, and strange beasts
and an old vet in a winey tunic
slipping on the slop that covers cobblestones,
and carpenters carrying planks
of fresh-cut timbers shouting Out the Way,
and stores with the finest silk from Cos
and lotions from Libya, furs from the north,
the latest shoes and scarfs (mostly knockoffs).
There are wine shops, butchers, silversmiths,
tailors, book dealers, peddlers
peddling rags and knives and amulets,
fresh cod and marinated eels
and rancid fish raised in the drains.

There's more to Rome than Subura
of course, but that's another letter.

Paccia explains why she left

Dear Caius,
I said I would,
so here's the story of my leaving.
But before I tell it, let me say
I loved you, loved you more
than you could comprehend.
You woke me to the world
and I woke you to love.
I loved you and there were no others.
As you surmised, others tried: Sustio
and that other friend, the preachy one,
but never Glabbis, he loved you too
and never would. He read your poems to me
that troubled me, your doubts and fears,
and also women that you'd had, a black girl
and a pleb and that Perenice.
I thought I was just another one in line.

And you shouldn't have made fun of my doll.
My mother made her, in the skirt and headdress
of our patron-saint to protect me in the world.
I brought her here with me
and she has served me well.
My daughter has her by her bed,
tattered now, providing comfort.

I am a mother, Caius. I didn't know that's what
I wanted. Chance and choice are easily confused
but when she kissed my cheek
like a baby chick, I knew then
and when he, thinking it close,

reached for the moon, my heart leapt.
I sacrificed my art to raise them
for it isn't art that lasts, it's flesh,
children and their children.

You got some things about me right,
brown hazel eyes, long legs,
but you had a strange way of praising me,
hair like coal, pungent olive skin,
a snide remark about a scarf to hide my neck:
you didn't miss a thing,
but no, I was never naked under my dress,
even on the hottest nights.

My own fault. I wanted you to think me wild,
a peregrine, untrained, a native of the hills,
an image I invented for your pleasure when in fact
my father was the mayor and knew the law and Latin.
I wasn't running up goat paths to sing
among the birds or carting wool,
but learning about the Turdetani past
and Roman ways and how the gypsies
sang and danced.

When you thought you'd lost me
you chiseled at my feelings
with empty words of love.
When a woman loves a man,
it is a sea, not words.
It is a mountainside of firs
not words.
It is with her heart, Caius
not with words.

Paccia relates a dream to Caius

I dreamed we sailed
with fourteen rowers who were barely needed,
the wind drove us south to Lixus
where we climbed a hill and watched the sun sink
into the sea and the evening star rise.
Then I dreamed of those lovely girls,
how Hera didn't trust them
not to eat the golden apples
and set down a many-headed dragon to guard her fruit.
The girls had arms as white as snow
and golden hair. They sang with limpid voices
while they ate the fruit
that came in segments and was sweet.
With that, I woke, and thought of you,
the way we ate black olives by the stream.

Lycoris

Lycoris informs Gallus

You ask, how are you? It's like a shriek.
Love me. Love me.
Be consoled, Gallus, I'm an actress who, on stage,
am everything and nothing, a beauty, witch,
girl, hag. I tell lewd jokes and sing songs
worthy of the sirens. To be myself is too exhausting
but with you I was not acting.
My love was real.

That's over now.
But don't be sad.
You and I will live forever in your poems.
Four books! And I am center stage in every one.
Don't listen to the critics who call them lumpish
and complain of their flat diction.
It was your songs I fell for first,
their passion and their music.
But you'd have me live in Egypt?
Dearie, please.

LEUCONOE, LYDIA, CHLOE,
LALAGE, PHYLLIS, VENUS,
LYCE, PYRRHA, AND ASTERIE

Leuconoe tells Horace to enjoy the present

Don't ask, Quintus, what the gods plan for you or me,
    they don't want it known;
gods are gods because they don't think
    of anything but being.
Don't mess around with auguries and horoscopes.
    It's better to accept whatever comes,
whether it be many winters or one last naked summer.
    Time is short so curtail all hope
 and drink your wine. Each moment wants our praise.
    Embrace the day
and leave tomorrow for another time.

Lydia and Horace having one of their quarrels

        You know Lydia
when you loved me
        and loved the way
        I kissed your ivory neck
I was happy as a Persian prince
                if not as rich.

        Yes I know
but that was when you burned for me
        and not for Chloe.
        I was on top, more triumphant
than a Roman princess
                if not as pure.

        It's true,
Chloe is a learnéd girl who sings
        the sweetest notes
        and moves in artful ways.
                I'd die for her to save her life.

        That boy Calais
who I burn for, who burns for me,
        shines brighter than the brightest star.
                I'd die *twice* for him
                        to spare *his* life.

        Lydia, stop a moment,
let's imagine Chloe out the door
        and you and I, two strays
        who've wandered home
and find the door is open.
                I'll wear the leash of love again.

Quintus, listen,
Calais is sweet and honest,
    while you're a cork
            bobbing on the sea,
but I would love to live with you again
        and with you love again
                and gladly "die"

Lalage says be patient

I'm a filly not a mare,
so cannot bear a stallion's plunge.
I tremble like young leaves in spring
or tender grapes alarmed by sun and rain,
not yet a blue cluster in full fruit.
Besides, it's said a girl in flight is beautiful.
I'll be eager for you when I have more years,
my shoulders gleaming white and milky
as the full moon shining on the sea.

Phyllis responds to Horace's invitation

It sounds lovely, casks of well-aged Alban wine
and fresh ivy I can use to bind my hair.
Servant girls and boys running all over making
the house shine, a perfect party
in honor of your patron's birthday.
And you, so sweet to say I'm your last love,
there'll be no other. I believe you, but
            I can't come

because a girl must aim high
and I've learned songs to sing to Telephus
and when he hears my lovely voice
he'll dump that young rich girl
who has him in her claws
and realize that his love for me,
and mine for him is richer
            than her riches.

Venus confirms Horace's fears

Okay Flaccus, I'll spare you
for you're not the man you were
when you loved young Cinara,
who was so lovely, who could resist her?
But she's long gone, and you are fifty,
too stiff to bow to love's demands
and short. And fat.

I'll go to where I'm needed,
in my chariot pulled by swans (that you call geese)
and warm the heart of Paulus, he is young
and rich and wellborn, handsome too,
and more than ready to be toasted on both sides.

I know that you no longer care for such things.
A tear appears out of nowhere and drips
down your nose and splashes on your lip.
You start to speak, no words come
(you used to be so glib).
You meet a friend whose name you don't remember
or both name and face escape you.
Now it is in dreams you lust,
you hold her warm and gentle
and in your sleep you almost love again.

Lyce resists Horace

I'm not moved by gifts or prayers
        so let it go.
Even if I were married to some lout
in a foreign land and bored,
        I'd resist you.

You say it's love.
Are you sure it's not malaria?
Try some Silphium from Cyrene,
its juice reverses baldness
        and helps digestion.

You think I'm cruel; I'm just sensible.
Venus doesn't like persistence.
My father raised me like that wife who spun
and wept and waited, rejecting all
        unsuitable suitors.

Lyce gives up on love

No more words, vapid, tired words
that slice like a knife.
I'd stick a needle through his tongue
to stop him talking, making words
that I once waited for.
No more avoiding his gaze,
his glassy eyes bugging out with desire.

Not for me, the same meal for the thousandth time,
the same song tugging at my heart
like someone plucking weeds.
No, now the solitary act,
    it's enough.

Lyce finds true love

You came when I was
        longing for you.
As if you knew,
        you came
and stirred me like a strong wind.

You came and looked at me
        and wove flowers
in a garland
        in my hair.

You said: there's no need to worry.
        Let it come naturally

and my desire for you,
        in our bed,
                was sated.

Lyce and her friend

Tell everyone
      sing of her figure,
slim and fragrant,
      graceful,
because Sappho says the evening star's
      the most beautiful.

I ask only that when we go out
      she wear the white dress
and when we walk on the beach,
      we make love right there,
         on the gleaming stones
               polished by the sea.

Lyce's difficult girlfriend

Now you hide from me like stars
from the full moon.
You shut yourself in your room.
If you don't come out
I won't love you,
won't praise the way you wear
bright bracelets
and those eccentric shoes.
I won't caress your girlish limbs.

Pyrrha answers Horace

Which slight youth
seeped in cologne
Pyrrha
brings you roses
to your rented rooms
 and gets to kiss you?

I invited up that slim youth
and taught him how to wear his perfume,
not too much, and taught him
            how to love.

Do you, as before,
slip into something basic
and tie back
your shining hair?

I slip into something elegant
and wear one ribbon (two's too many).
I dazzle that young man
            with my golden hair.

Eager, inept,
so dazzled by your glow –
does he think that you are true?

Yes he thinks that I am true
            and yes I am.
You wouldn't understand
            such love.
We wed a month ago
            and live as one.

Asterie weeps for her husband

I weep for him, detained in Greece by eastern winds.
I know that he'll return in springtime with his cargo
and I know he spends cold nights crying out for me
and doesn't listen to the daughter of the tavern
who tells him stories of unfaithful wives.

Which is unfair.
I do wait faithfully
and am not tempted
by my neighbor's son
and hardly notice how
he breaks young horses
in the morning
and walking past the herons
on the mudflats
plunges into the Tiber
and swims across and back.
I don't listen
to his plaintive flute.
I am as stone,
deaf and blind,
and lock my door at night.

Asterie, divorced, pledges her love (to her neighbor's son)

Why, if his heart was as hard as stone
and his limbs as flabby as an eel's
and his father was a farmhand
and I myself a lowly slave –
if all of that were true,
I'd still be his, and let him know
he is my joy, my life,
and I am sure he'd say the same.

Lydia tells Horace

You thought I was the kind
you could forget and I'd go off
and sob and whine in a corner

get bitten by a viper to die
a sickly death or ask a witch for a magic
potion, a cup of poisoned wine
to send to you, a gift.

Damned if you'll get one sign
of my unhappiness.
I swear it by the gods
and wondrous icons
you'll not see me weep
or beg. As for your hope
that you so long for,
that I come back to you:
Fat chance.

Lydia refutes Horace's curse

You say I'll end up in an alley on moonless nights
with married men, a frenzied mare in heat.
It's true, young men don't throw pebbles
at my window hoping for some love
or fly to me like furry moths to flame
or whisper syrup words that make me swell.

But I'm no dry leaf, no old rag, I have a lover
who's a man. We summer in the Alban Hills
and spend winter in the city.
We celebrate feast days with old wine
and read the Georgics in the evening by the fire
and make love without theatrics.

Horace's women, a chorus.

Flaccus, listen, do not worry, we all love you.
    Pyrrha, blond and elegant, offers you her heart.
Lydia, naughty, has agreed to light your fire.
    Lyce says she'll do it one more time.
Phyllis could not make it,
she is off with Telephus
        but sends her love.
Lalage is finally ready and is trembling
        with laughter.
Asterie's pissed about you doubting her fidelity
        but forgives you.

We are many, we are one, phantom names
        so you can fill
            your poetry with females
                good and bad and always festive.

Corinna, Cypássis, Marcia and Perilla

Corinna at a dinner party with Ovid

I'll be there early – why? No reason.
But you however wait until he's there.
Yes my husband will be there
so don't come early, and when you do,
mingle with the other guests.
Once we're seated, you can only look,
don't touch. Not once. And after too much wine,
if he flings his arm around me and tries
to touch my breast, try not to groan.
He likes to sneak a hand beneath my top;
I won't let him and I won't allow his kiss
or if I do just one, all the rest are yours.
Just restrain yourself. I'll try to nudge
your foot with mine. Observe my nods and winks.
Who needs words? If you are thinking
of us in the act, tug gently on your ear.
I'll then slide my ring around.
I'll encourage him to drink and if he passes out
we'll plan on when to meet and where.

Corinna visits Ovid

It was hot, the hottest part of the day,
around two or three when I went in,
the shutters closed because he thinks
I like it dim, but light
filtered through like light through trees

and I looked fine, hair tumbled down
in such a way to show my long white neck,
and he, already half undressed
tore at my dress careful not to tear it,
and I fought to keep it on, careful not to do so.
I melted like a wax doll in the sun
and stood there naked, and we both admired
my breasts, flat belly, wide hips,
still youthful thighs, my face a little thin
but overall a masterpiece of exercise and diet.
He bared his teeth as if to rip my flesh
and me, open, open . . .

You can imagine the rest.
Exhausted, sweaty, we lay down and slept.
Please, may there be more afternoons like that one.

Corinna accuses Ovid

You, choose a wretched slave? Never!
Consort with a servant? Heavens no!
You would never think of such a thing,
you, a cross-eyed lying drunk,
congratulations, you're a self-made man.

You fool. Cypássis told me everything.
Besides, I knew – I could smell her on you.
So I said, Cypássis, you can tell me, how was it,
and she blushed and stumbled over a reply.

Lady, he threatened to betray me, he,
trained in legal words, threatened
to blame me for the thing we did, hurried,
in the dark where he couldn't see how dark
my skin is. He caressed the scars on my back
from where you had me whipped that other time,
with the man whose name I'm not to say.
Never in your bed I swear, not once,
always in the back room, in the dark,
no soft words or kisses or if kisses,
kisses smelling of that musty wine he drinks.
No, just the act and it was quick, a few times.

Marcia writes to her husband Ovid in exile

Naso, dear, I miss you so, I miss your laughter
in the kitchen; our three remaining servants
            have no sense of humor.
I miss you in our barren bedroom,
your plumpness next to mine at night.
I miss your feet and tender quips.
            I am a silly girl.

Most of all I miss our gossiping about the royals
and how He sent his daughter off in exile to an island
and then *her* daughter to another island
            where she had a baby
that He ordered to be thrown
onto a garbage heap for wolves or slavers.
            The innocent, what fate is that?
The gods decide or is it He, who thinks he is a god.

The gossip now, spread as rumor by your rivals,
that you are still in Rome sulking in a villa
            on the outskirts writing verse,
an anti-epic about a mewling poet
exiled in a northern town who mocks the Princeps.
The story is that you will spring it on the public
after He is gone and thus ensure your fame.

Your fame is not in jeopardy, my dear.
It's true, He's banned *Amores* from the libraries
but your poems live on, read by all
who value eloquence and elegance and wit.

Marcia cautions Ovid

Dear Husband,
You call me good. I do my best. I send our pleas
and sorrows to His friends and cousins.
You needn't tell me how to grovel
for I'm an expert at it now.
I've done as you requested,
suggested that He move you to a warmer place,
further south, say Smyrna with its baths
and gardens where speech is Greek and Latin,
lovely Smyrna which the Emperor
might one day visit,
      or Ephesus, either one.

But dear, I have to tell you that
your letters do not help.
They are overworked like horses raced too often.
There's too much whining mixed with flattery,
an overkill of praise, malice and cold respect.
Your pal Propertius praises them in private
      but rips them at the clubs.

I fear your oblique insults may provoke Him
and we've seen what gods and kings can do,
to punish for the slightest lapse.
They enjoy it. It defines them.
Not just honest power, we grant them that,
but arbitrary power, that's what makes them squirm
with pleasure. Defy them and they just get mad.
In the end we kneel down at the shrine of random force,
struck blind, shouting
      I deserve it, I repent, I repent.

Marcia ponders why her husband was exiled

He writes me, says it was the wine,
something he said, a careless error,
          a mere mistake, not a crime.
Augustus claims it was *Amores*,
those early love poems, naughty stuff,
a joke (but not a good one).
My Naso never did those steamy things,
his poems were far more wanton than his life,
but His daughter loved them
and tried to live that life.

No, it wasn't Art that caused his ruin
for poems are nothing in the face of Power.
I think it was his poking fun at prudist laws
          and dumb reforms
(unlike Virgil and young Horace paying court
          to Him and his regime).
My man compared war to war between the sexes
and said that the empire was spreading like a stain.

Some say it's what he saw or overheard,
words of treason, a whispered plot.
Did he wish Him gone? Of course,
          half the city did.

I think He just disliked him, disliked and envied.
Successful early, reckless with the truth,
a bit too bawdy (says the Hypocrite in Chief
who sneaks out for the girls),
my man was what He wished to be,
and so He hated and he loved in equal portions,
apologies to Catullus, who if he'd lived
would be in Tomis with my poet.
What a pair they'd make, mixing anguish
in their cups with pure hilarity.

Marcia sends her daughter Perilla to Tomis

I know you suffer, Naso
and I wish that I could come
but I am needed here to plead your case.
I am sending Perilla. She wants to go
and learn from you the art of poetry.
An earnest girl, she hopes to please you
with her verses. You can guide her
on the use of myths and polymetrics,
you're so good at both,
but don't go on forever, as you tend to do,
and don't dear overdo the wit,
it harms the overall effect.
She's smart and thoughtful, our Perilla,
and she loves you like a daughter.

Perilla writes to her mother from Tomis

Dearest Mother,
After nearly a year here, I can say it's true,
what Naso has said, Tomis is a town of mud
and lumber, a harsh grim place. When wine freezes
we break it off in chunks to drink.
The sea is greasy. Fur-clad, long-haired nomads
cross the frozen Danube in their creaking wagons
with long-range arrows tipped with venom
strapped across their backs, to raid
in a marauding swath for grain,
goats, women, children.
Thank the gods that Roman soldiers backed by locals
drive them off.

But spring is lovely. The tyrant sea, tinted green,
gives up its cold, fledglings squawk in nests
and swallows bicker under eaves,
the first green tender stalks poke through
the soil, boughs fill with blossoms, grapes
cluster beneath thick leaves.

Summer days are hot and sunny, with a gentle breeze
flowing off the sea, nights are warm and somewhat muggy.
Trees bear fruit above the names of lovers etched in bark.
We go bathing in the sea or to mineral springs to soak.
Native women scrub us down and we return refreshed.

Autumn too is warm, the earth is dark and rich
in corn and wheat, richer still in grapes and olive;
froth tops the vats, and children run through town
shouting on their way to school.

The town has servant girls singing as they spin,
shepherds playing flutes to soothe their flocks,
a small band playing tunes, rough but pleasing,
in the evening. Naso sits in cafés,
plays chess, writes his next epistle,
gossips with ship captains,
practices the local Black Sea tongues with natives
who have drifted in, tough tribesmen
brave, sturdy, honest with their own strong moral code.

But he won't admit all this in letters.
He says that if he hinted life is not so bad
Augustus would prolong his exile, thinking that he
has it good, or send him further north
where hordes of nomads swarm the steppe
like buzzing hornets.

Perilla on writing poetry

Because Latin is a supple tool that spurs the mind
to say what's true and what is not,
I spend most days writing and it saves me
from despair. Recording life and manners,
mulling over thoughts and feelings, matching
sounds to meaning, manipulating meters so they fit
the sense, choosing just the image that describes
the surface and the essence of a thing,
throwing in a myth that illustrates the point.
The time goes quickly, when I write.
It's been this way since I was twelve.

Perilla on Beauty

Men fall hard for it
but why rejoice in beauty?
It's paid in adoration
that lasts a summer.
They prize it far above what women do.
It wins hearts, hearts that fade,
flowers on the forest floor.
Like Narcissus looking into water
beauty sees itself and drowns.
What in all the world's as vain
and ushers in such grief?

Perilla and the monkey

It was a hot, a boiling day
without a cloud or breeze
and I was walking in the street
and saw a gypsy of some sort
sitting on the ground.
Above him, on a wall, a monkey dressed
in a red skirt and orange blouse
was drinking from a saucer. She bent
her balding head to the dish, her back
arched high above her,
and drank greedily. Around her neck,
a leather collar with a chain
that led to the ragged man below.
She seized the dish and swept it off the wall,
then seeing me, she rose, and offered me her
black wet little hand.
It was a gentle gesture.
Mother, I have shaken hands with poets,
well-born, senators but never once like this,
filled with dignity and grace and sweetness.
She gazed into my eyes with such sorrow
and affection, even wisdom, that in recognition
of our sisterhood, I yearned to set her free.
In that moment a cloud crept across the sun,
a sultry thunder clapped.
The gypsy rose, brushed off his pants,
thumped his tambourine, and walked off,
the monkey rocking rhythmically
on his shoulder, and I decided then,
it was time to return to Rome,
it was time to come home.

Perilla's poem about Ariadne

Waking on the beach, stirring, still sleepy
my hand reached out for you
and there was nothing.
I turned over and reached out
and nothing, no one there.
And moved my arm across where you had been
and groped the empty air.

I ran a little way, my feet dragged
down by heavy sand
and back
and up the beach,
treading in your footprints,
shouting out your name
    Theseus
and the cliff responded in a languid echo
    see-us
as if the place itself cried out for you.

I climbed a hill and it was then
I saw the southern wind stretch the sail.
Wait, I shrieked and waved my arms
thinking you would see me
and realize that you'd left your love behind.
    Wait!
and beat my chest
    Come back!
  the words and blows in rhythm.
I shouted one last time.
The ship sailed on, a shrinking speck
beneath the sky, swallowed
by the mild blue vapor.

Now first frost coats the ground like scattered glass,
birds hidden in the trees lament the coming of the cold.
I see no people, cattle, cultivated fields,
                    just sea, a sea without a sail.
And if there were a sail, where would I go?
Not back to Crete, to the father I betrayed
or Athens where I'd find you boasting of your exploits.
You should have killed me with the bull
who was despite your lies a gentle creature.

Now I fear more than I grieve. I fear the serpents
who will sting me and the lions who will tear my flesh.
You left me here to die alone,
for death to scatter first my soul, then my bones.

Perilla's poem about Ariadne and death

Death was there, on the beach,
  her hair tied in a rag, singing

    She saw me, shrugged.

I said, you can have my song,
you can have my body
  you can have my sorrow

    She heard me and just shrugged

      and that was that.

DOORS

Lesbia's door
She tells me let him in,
he's a *famous* poet.
In other words, keep my mouth shut.

Sulpicia's door in Rome
She's gone to Arretium
and if a door could weep
I'd weep.

Her door in Arretium
I don't bother with a bolt.
Who would steal jars of honey
or flagons of wine?

Phohoe'
She tells me watch who comes with gifts
and let him in; if none, then don't.

Nemesis'
I'm always off the latch
just push me open.
You are welcome any time.

Cynthia's
She says be selective
but how tell a poet from a rogue?
They all display a sad and avid visage
and if they get a foot in they want more.

Lalage's
Horace is homely
but he speaks so well.
When I'm older
I'll swing on my hinges for him
like a leaping dolphin.

Lyce's
I wouldn't even let you lie down on my doorstep
to listen to me creak in the wind.

Lydia's
I'll undo the lock, open just wide enough
for even fatso to slip through.

Corinna's
Now that Naso's married to Marcia
he never comes around.
It's just as well.

Phyllis'
Stand out there all you want
weeping, pleading, hopping on one foot.
If a door could laugh I'd laugh.

Perilla's
I am shut to you and any man
who thinks she's less than virtuous.

# AND ONE GREEK

La Circe

Circe, that's me. It's pronounced Keer Key.
You've heard the stories, that I lived alone
and changed his men to swine and how he loved me
for a year until I sent him off to Hades.
It was not for punishment but because he liked
to wander and dreaded going back to Ithaca
and that lovely wife who was, let's be frank, a bore.

I moved to Athens; it was crowded; then to Paris,
which was filthy. I waited there for him to tire
of his patient wife and when that didn't happen,
I moved to Rome which is where you find me.

It's true, I turned his men to swine. I don't know why
I do those things. Lonely. Pride I guess. Bitter.
For although my Father was the Sun and Mom
the daughter of the Sea, (and my sister was the Queen
of Crete where she played around with acrobats
and fucked a bull!), Dad called me Goat
and cast me out but gave me guile
and witchcraft and a rapid mind.

I landed on an island with a bunch of witless nymphs.
It seemed forever, 'til his men showed up,
came up the hill and shouted at my door
as if I were a servant. "Come in," I said and gave them
meat and mead, my special mead. They were gluttonous
and ignorant so I confirmed them in their nature,
bestowed upon them bristles, snouts and grunts
but left their human minds intact for otherwise
they'd just love the life a pig lives,
eating mash and wallowing in mud.

What followed was amazing.
I told Homer how that sailor wandered in here
like a lout and ate and drank, a clever devil
who knew my tricks and used them to seduce me.
And I him. The nymphs did all the rest
with baths and oils and roasts and wine
and afterward, a finger bowl.

I liked his back. It was broad and scarred
and supple as the sea, but there was something
else I can't define: not his wit, which turned out
to be stock, or his cunning, although he truly
was a man of twists and turns. No,
there was something hidden, a weakness
which he himself didn't understand,
almost like a shyness, a willingness
to wonder, an excitement, that led to, in my hands,
a revelation for us both: he was a boy,
a boy I loved. and I a girl who loved.

Four seasons wheeled across the island
before he tired of the baths and love.
There became a darkness to our love,
he an egoist and I half mad with anger.
When war erupted, in bed and out,
he brooded on the shore, looking west.
I had to let him go.

And Homer soaked it up and wrote of us.
The whole world followed, poets each
with different slants. I got a good
review from Ovid, bless his rotten soul,
'til he went off the rails and called me
Queen of Lust and made up that story

about me changing Picus to a woodpecker.
Plutarch said his men were better off as pigs.
Boccaccio called me forceful, eloquent
but not overly concerned with virtue
(of his hundred famous women
he included me but left off Calypso
who really was a witch).
There were many others: J. Joyce labeled me
a madam with a Jewish name. Fellini filmed me,
the Sophia played me and the Red Brigades
paid me for a moment of my time,
to be their symbol of eternally exploited female.

The English weren't content with Greek.
Chapman called and asked if Elpenor fell off the roof
by accident or did I do it, to remind my man
to watch his step. Pope chimed in and spoke
in couplets. As for Lattimore, I asked him
why he called my bed beautiful but not a word
of praise for me. He mumbled something.
Fitzgerald fell for me, called me dire beauty and divine,
said I had a beguiling voice, compared me to a cat.
It was Fagles who wondered if the sex was good,
did Odysseus bring me pleasure, was it raunchy
or conventional? (I think Fagles was inflamed).
T.E. never called; I'm not his type
and dear young Sarah Ruden sent a telegram,
"Stuck in Aeneid. Stop. Will be in touch. Stop."

I don't know why they bother. Homer did it better
for all time, although I have to say his Greek
is wondrous strange, rapid, plain and noble all at once.
He understood his heroes were not real,
his stories not written for the classroom
but for cash and lamb and wine.

So life goes on. That's what I told the man
who shared my bed and loved and left.
He lives in books; I in Rome, in a district
called Testaccio, once a marketplace and slaughterhouse,
now it's trendy gourmet food stores, boutiques
and high-rise condos for the oldest families
and a few stray ageless gods. Yes I'm ageless,
but even ageless I am getting old and tired.
I take my meds, play Gin against my Mac
and watch the news about Berlusconi and his whores.
My weavings had a modest show and sold a few.
I wouldn't change a thing. I rarely use my wand.

In certain moments, when the air is mild,
I recall our nights of love, his voice and looks,
his hands, immense and gentle, and the way
he held me in them, like a bird, careful
not to harm me, but when they touched me
they alarmed me, sent a shock like phosphorous
across my body. Now I sigh, and know
that he lives only in the minds
of others, and although he loved me,
being mortal he's forgotten me, his Circe.

THE WOMEN

Lesbia

Lesbia, the woman loved and hated by Catullus, was in all probability Clodia Metelli, a woman born into one of the highest aristocratic families of Rome. She was married to a powerful statesman and was ten years older than Catullus. It has been suggested that she wrote poetry but no poems have been found. She is portrayed by history, based on Cicero's denunciation of her at a trial, as an alcoholic tramp, promiscuous and possibly incestuous. I portray her, however, as a complex woman who genuinely loves Catullus but is ready to move on if events warrant it. Sophisticated, proud of her ancestry, jaded, vain about her looks but self-conscious about her age, she is a good poet but considers it a pastime.

Delia, Nemesis and Prohoe

Delia is addressed by Tibullus as a beautiful love object but I have depicted her as a clever, lighthearted and tolerant young woman who is a good pal to Tibullus. She realizes that Tibullus is gay, something which is suggested by his poetry but not substantiated by history. She also realizes that she is not a real woman and has been created by Tibullus for literary purposes.

Nemesis is another of Tibullus' lovers, equally elusive. We don't know why he gave her the name Nemesis, but I have taken the hint and revealed her to be fate or necessity. As such she is a tough cookie, relentless and implacable, the equivalent of Freud's reality principle.

Phohoe is a courtesan, probably Greek, and cynical about love. Sarcastic, erotic but loveless, she is droll about her calculations.

Sulpicia

Sulpicia was a real person, the only female Roman poet whose works have survived. We know little about her life. In one poem she refers to herself rather formally as Svlpicia Servi Filia, the daughter of Servius, but we don't know who he was. In several of her poems she mentions her uncle and guardian Valerius Messalla Corvinus, a prominent statesman and patron of the arts. Her six short poems, totaling forty lines in all, survived as part of the *Corpus Tibullianum,* a collection of poems by Tibullus and other poets affiliated with her uncle.

In the six poems that I have added to her work, I have portrayed her as naïve and petulant, but with a fresh spontaneous voice. She takes her craft seriously. After falling for a farmer's son, she is passionate and proud of her sexuality and a bit melodramatic.

Cynthia

Cynthia was the object of Propertius' obsession and was probably based on a real woman named Hostia, but who Hostia was we don't know. In his poems the two of them run hot and cold. She is described as wanton and vengeful, almost a sadist to his self-pitying masochist. My Cynthia is self-conscious of her dubious social status and can be angry and bitter, but she is also tempestuous and funny and as such, well matched with Propertius.

Paccia

Paccia Glycera was the lover of Caius Herennius Felix, both of whom are fictional characters in my book *The Poems of Caius Herennius Felix.* In that book she is one of the famous dancing girls of Cadiz and is unpredictable and sly and more interested in money than in love. Herennius, it turns out, badly misread her. Now she is in Rome, a loving wife and mother. Her children, however, are nearly grown and her thoughts have drifted back to her wild life in Cadiz and her lover.

Lycoris

Lycoris was the pseudonym for a real and famous Roman actress named Volumnia Cytheris, a freedwoman who had an affair with the poet Gallus, then with Brutus followed by a long affair with Marc Antony until he dumped her for Cleopatra. She is fond of Gallus but doesn't take him seriously. Being an actress, perhaps she lacks a core identity, something that may have appealed to the feckless Antony.

Leuconoe. Lydia, Chloe, Lalage, Phyllis, Lyce, Pyrrha, Asterie

All these women are mentioned or addressed in the poems of Horace, but he doesn't individualize them and scholars have been unable to identify any of them. It is possible that some or all of them are simply names used by Horace to suit the genre of love poem.

I have attempted to give them distinctive personalities. Leuconoe is the young woman to whom Horace addressed his famous *carpe diem* (seize the day) poem. Her name is a compound of two Greek words, *leukos*, pallid, and *nous*, mind, and may be roughly translated as empty headed. In my poem, she turns the tables on Horace and tells *him* to pluck the day.

Lydia is feisty, amorous, playful, a match for Horace. Of all of Horace's women, I think she was a real person. She gives up on him and settles down with a more mature and trustworthy lover.

Chloe is one of Horace's young lovers. He mentions her in four poems but it is not clear if she is always the same person. In my poem, she is *a learnéd girl who sings the sweetest note and moves in artful ways.*

Lalage is young, shy, modest, and afraid of men.

Phyllis is a straightforward young woman with a practical side and hopes for an advantageous marriage.

Lyce calls herself sensible. She is out of sorts and is fed up with men, gives up sex, is slow to realize she is gay, but once she falls in love she is erotic and sensuous.

Pyrrha is a courtesan with wit who decides to marry her young and well-off lover.

Asterie is a loving but somewhat dim wife whose thoughts are straying to her neighbor's son. After her divorce, she proclaims her love for the new lover in stock language.

Corinna, Cypássis Marcia and Perilla

Ovid addressed poems to his mistress Corinna, wrote letters in verse to his wife, and mentioned his stepdaughter Perilla once.

Corinna is a married woman having affairs with poets; she is devious, lusty, and just as amoral as Ovid.

Cypássis is a slave from north Africa, a lot more sexual than she lets on, and doesn't lie well.

Marcia, Ovid's third wife, is at times sentimental but is rock solid, pragmatic, loyal, and wise. Although Ovid wrote many letters to her, he never gives us her name. I give her the name Marcia.

Perilla is referred by Ovid as his stepdaughter, Marcia's dutiful daughter. She is a poet, but that is all we know. I have imagined her as sensitive, observant, ambitious, and a serious artist.

Doors

Doors play a prominent part in Latin poetry. Poets languish outside them hoping to be allowed in to be with their lovers. My doors write epigrams.

Circe

Circe, part human, part goddess, is Greek, worldly, well-read, and resourceful, yet capable of wonder and love. She still lives in Rome.

THE POEMS

Lest readers be confused about the authorship of these poems, Jim Levy wrote them all, but many images and phrases are taken from existing poems by the famous male Latin poets. Also, some poems are adaptations of existing poems from non-Latin sources. Sulpicia's lament about her lover's leaving for the army has phrases from an 18th century Irish ballad. Perilla on beauty borrows from *Reflections* by Madame Deshoulières and her poem about a monkey is an adaptation of a poem by Vladislav Khodasevich. *Cynthia goads Propertius* is adapted loosely from a poem by Cecco Angiolieri and *Sulpicia and her love* is adapted from a poem by Heinrich von Morungen.

Acknowledgements

My thanks to Christina Haas at Zenith Publishing Solutions for formatting this book and designing the cover.

I was greatly aided and encouraged by A. S. Kline, the creator of the web site Poetry in Translation. His translations from the Latin, (as well as from Chinese, Greek, Italian, French, German, Spanish, Russian, and others) were a major resource and he himself a consistent support and inspiration.

I wish to thank the women in my life, colleagues, bosses, friends, lovers, wives and family, from whom I have learned what little I understand about women.

ABOUT THE AUTHOR

Jim Levy grew up in Los Angeles and Taos, New Mexico and is the son of a Freudian psychoanalyst and a mother who aspired to be a writer. He worked for forty years as an executive for nonprofit organizations and has published ten books of essays, memoirs, poetry and travel. Although he took two years of Latin at the Thacher School in Ojai, California, he spent most classes hiding behind the teacher's dog Patroclus and he knows no Latin.

He can be reached at jimlevy40@gmail.com.

9 781733 794039